# In Christ

# Alone

## Discovering Your
## Identity In  Christ

**Tom Lemler**

In Christ Alone:
Discovering Your Identity In Christ

Tom Lemler
Impact Prayer Ministry
2730 S Ironwood Dr
South Bend IN 46614
www.impactprayerministry.com
tlemler@gapministry.com

Cover Photo by MJ Lemler

As I spent time with God listening for direction in writing the weekly Lifestyle of Prayer guides to start the new year, He kept reminding me of a list of Bible verses I had been given dealing with what we have in Christ. That list turned into five weekly prayer guides and then into the skeleton for this book. I pray that the content and design of this book helps you to grow in your discovery of who you are in Christ.

This book is dedicated in grateful acknowledgment to God who has given me an incredible identity through His Son, Jesus. I also thank Suzanne Lee who initially gave me the list of scriptures with the request that I do something with them to help the Deer Run congregation have a better understanding of their identity in Christ. I thank my wife and daughter for their encouragement and support, as well as my co-workers and elders at the Deer Run Church of Christ who greatly encourage and support the work I do with Impact Prayer Ministry. To all of these, and to you my readers, thank you!

# Table of Contents

**In Christ . . .**

## Introduction

Who am I?  This is an age-old question that many people ask, often never sure how to fully find an answer.  Through time in prayer, this book was written to help you spend time with God discovering who He says you are in Christ! This book will take you on a prayer-filled journey as you examine some of what the Bible says you have and/or are in Christ.

You may use this book as a thirty-one day devotional or go through it at whatever pace suits you.  I would recommend that you don't rush it.  Take your time to let each statement about your identity in Christ sink in deep within you.  The book is designed to be used as both a devotional and a journal as you discover what God says about you.

Each topic follows the same three-page format.  The first page is simply a statement of that day's identity focus and a scripture reference to get you started in God's Word. Spend time wearing that statement as part of your identity and see how it looks on you! Look up the scripture reference and meditate on God's Word about who you are in Christ.

The second page is some devotional writing that has come from my prayer time focused on that day's subject. It will include questions to help you think more clearly about how God sees you. There will be direction and suggestions on how to focus your prayer time as you seek to grow in that area of identity. As you go through this page of each day's topic, spend time with God in prayer for yourself and for the people around you to have a greater grasp of who we are in Christ.

The third page is your turn to make this devotional even more personal! It contains a heading of the day's topic and then a blank lined page. This is for you to record your interaction with God each day. Jot down your thoughts, your prayers, other scriptures that God brings to mind during your time with Him, and/or changes in your attitude or actions that He reveals you need to make. Use this journal page to help you remember and to help you grow.

In prayer,
Tom Lemler
Impact Prayer Ministry

Day One

# In Christ

# I Have Peace

(Romans 5: 1)

### I Have Peace.

How would you rate your level of peace today? What factors determine if you feel a sense of peace or not? Some have described peace as the absence of conflict, but does living without conflict always lead to a life of true peace? Could the peace you long for, the peace beyond understanding, be something more — a peace that could exist even in the midst of conflict?

God says that in Christ we have peace because we have been made right with God through our faith in Jesus! Our prayer life should draw us into greater peace as our faith in God grows. As you grow in Christ, pray that you would live as one justified by faith so that the people around you can see the peace you have in Christ. Pray that your inner peace would be visible to all people, even in times of conflict. Pray that your identity of peace would lead you to be a peacemaker as you share about your faith in Jesus. Pray that the people around you would see the peace of God reflected in everything you do.

## *I Have Peace*.

_____

_____

_____

_____

_____

_____

_____

_____

_____

_____

_____

_____

_____

_____

_____

_____

_____

_____

Day Two

# In Christ
# I Am Dead
# to Sin

(Romans 6:2-3)

## I Am Dead to Sin.

What temptation is your greatest struggle? Is there any element of sin in your life that you have accepted as normal -- something you can't win against? Why do you think it still has some form of control over you? How would seeing yourself dead to that particular sin help you in your struggle to overcome it? What power does sin have over someone who is dead?

God says that all who have been immersed into Christ have been immersed into His death! Through Christ we have become dead to sin so that it no longer has power, or authority, over us. As you consider your identity in Christ, pray that you would overcome temptation through a recognition that you are dead to sin. Pray that you would be free from the grip of sin and its desire to lay hold of your life. Pray that you would continue to grow in a life that is dead to sin. Pray that the people around you would recognize you as one not controlled by sin. Pray that others would know a life that is dead to sin.

*I Am Dead to Sin*.

_____

_____

_____

_____

_____

_____

_____

_____

_____

_____

_____

_____

_____

_____

_____

_____

_____

_____

_____

Day Three

# In Christ
# I Have No
# Condemnation

(Romans 8:1)

## I Have No Condemnation.

What do you do when you feel the finger of condemnation pointed at you?  How does condemnation make you feel when you can think of nothing you have done wrong?  How about when you know you have been wrong?  How quick are you to condemn others for actions that you find repulsive?  How about for actions that you struggle with in your own life?

God says, and experience agrees, that every one of us have sinned.  When we are caught in our sin it often produces shame because of the condemnation we know we deserve.  In Christ, the penalty of sin has been paid so we are free from the condemnation that we deserve.  As you pray, ask God to free you from all traces of condemnation that the enemy tries to put on  you.  Pray that you would live as one free from condemnation because of Jesus.  Pray that the freedom from condemnation that you have in Christ would free you from having a condemning spirit toward others.  Pray for humility in living as one not condemned.

### *I Have No Condemnation*.

_____

_____

_____

_____

_____

_____

_____

_____

_____

_____

_____

_____

_____

_____

_____

_____

_____

_____

Day Four

# In Christ
# I Have Wisdom
# from God

(1 Corinthians 1:30)

## I Have Wisdom from God.

Have you ever done something only to realize afterwards that it was not a wise thing to do? Have you ever wrestled with how to have the wisdom to not do those things that are unwise? How would knowledge of both the source and result of wisdom help you make better decisions? What does having wisdom from God say about who you are? What does wisdom have to do with righteousness, holiness, and redemption?

God says that if we lack wisdom we should ask Him who gives freely. In Christ we have wisdom from God, Jesus Himself! As you pray, ask God to fill you with the presence of His wisdom in all areas of your life. Pray that you would use the wisdom that comes from God as He offers to give it freely to all who ask. Pray that you would understand more fully that the most true and important wisdom is found in the righteousness, holiness, and redemption that you have in Christ. Pray that the people around you would come to know Christ as the source of the only wisdom that is necessary for life.

## *I Have Wisdom From God.*

_____

_____

_____

_____

_____

_____

_____

_____

_____

_____

_____

_____

_____

_____

_____

_____

_____

_____

_____

_____

Day Five

# In Christ
# I Have
# God's Spirit

(1 Corinthians 2:12)

### I Have God's Spirit.

Do you struggle to understand the things of God and His Word? Do you ever wish there was someone always available to help you understand the gifting of God in your life? Do you have times when you feel lost in the ways of the world? How can you change when the ways of the world seem more natural to you than the ways of God? How often do you hear God's still small voice nudging you into the way you ought to go? More importantly, how often do you listen to that voice?

Most of us are bombarded daily with competing voices clamoring for us to do their will. We often struggle with clearly distinguishing God's voice from the voice of the enemy, and even from our own voice. As you pray today, ask God to make you more aware of His Spirit that lives within you. Pray that your life would be lived differently from those of the world because you have the Spirit of Christ in you. Pray for the eyes to see and ears to hear the things the Spirit says to you each day. Pray that the people around you would see the Spirit of God living in you.

## *I Have God's Spirit.*

_____

_____

_____

_____

_____

_____

_____

_____

_____

_____

_____

_____

_____

_____

_____

_____

_____

_____

Day Six

# In Christ
# I Have His
# Mind

*(1 Corinthians 2:16)*

## I Have the Mind of Christ.

Have you ever wished that you could crawl into the mind of someone so you would have a better understanding of how they think and who they are? Are you of the same mind with someone else to the extent that you can accurately finish sentences and thoughts of each other? Do you ever act like you know more than God? Does your life say that is so even if your words never would? What qualities should be most obvious in your life because you have the mind of Christ?

When we are in Christ, we should become so much like Christ that it is obvious that we have the mind of Christ! Our thoughts and words should be the same as we would expect from Christ. As you pray, ask God to fill you with a humility that allows you to be emptied of self and filled with the mind of Christ. Pray that your very thoughts, which determine your actions, would reflect the mind of Christ. Pray that your decisions would be based on what comes from the mind of Christ rather than from yourself. Pray that the people around you would see the mind of Christ in you.

*I Have the Mind of Christ.*

_____

_____

_____

_____

_____

_____

_____

_____

_____

_____

_____

_____

_____

_____

_____

_____

_____

_____

_____

Day Seven

# In Christ
# I Have Been
# Bought With
# a Price

(1 Corinthians 6:19-20)

### I Have Been Bought With a Price.

What is the most that you have ever paid for something? How does the price paid for something affect the way you treat it? How do you feel when someone else mistreats an item that you have purchased at great cost? What rights do you feel you have as a purchaser? How do you want your items treated that others borrow from you?

Most individuals and families that I know have at least one item of personal property that seems to be sacred to them. Do what you want to anything else and while there may be disappointment and sorrow, it is nothing compared to the heartache when that one item is damaged or destroyed. That is the level of extreme value that we have to God as we were bought with the incredible price of the blood of His Son, Jesus! As you pray, ask God to help you to always remember the price He paid for you. Pray that you would live in a way that honors the price Jesus has paid for you. Pray that you would share with others the value that God places on their life by His willingness to pay such a great price.

27

*I Have Been Bought With a Price.*

_____

_____

_____

_____

_____

_____

_____

_____

_____

_____

_____

_____

_____

_____

_____

_____

_____

_____

_____

Day Eight

# In Christ
# I Stand
# Firm

## (2 Corinthians 1:21-22)

### I Stand Firm.

How often do you feel like you are living the "one step forward, two step backward" way of life? Have you ever tried walking in conditions that were difficult or impossible to maintain solid footing? How much confidence do you gain when you have the proper footwear in icy or slippery conditions? What influence do product guarantees have on your trust of an item? What types of things might make a guarantee more believable or valuable to you?

At times life can seem to follow a treacherous and slippery path. With just a casual look around, most of us can see far too many people who have slipped and fallen along their chosen path. As you pray, ask God to always make you aware that He is the one who can make you stand firm in Christ. Pray that God's Spirit would help you to always stand firm in your faith. Pray that you would trust the guarantee that you have been given through the deposit of God's Spirit within you. Pray that your ability to stand firm in Christ, even in the midst of the instability of life, would draw others to Him.

## *I Stand Firm*.

_____

_____

_____

_____

_____

_____

_____

_____

_____

_____

_____

_____

_____

_____

_____

_____

_____

_____

*Day Nine*

# In Christ
# I Am a
# New Creation

## (2 Corinthians 5:17)

## I Am a New Creation.

What do you like the most about new things? What do you not like about new things? How easy/hard is it for you to take hold of new things if the old are still available to you? If there was one area of your life that you could make completely new, what would it be? What would it take to do so? Do you believe people can change? Do you believe you can change? Why or why not?

Many of us live with an internal tug-of-war where we like new things but are far more comfortable with many of the old things that define who we are. For example, I tend to buy new shoes but will rarely wear them until I actually throw the old ones out. As you pray, ask God to help you see any areas of your old life that you tend to cling to instead of claiming the new life that He gives. Pray that you would have the courage to always put away the old life and live as the new creation you are. Pray that you would trust God's ability to make not only you, but those around you, into a new creation when you are in Christ.

*I Am a New Creation*.

_____

_____

_____

_____

_____

_____

_____

_____

_____

_____

_____

_____

_____

_____

_____

_____

_____

_____

_____

*Day Ten*

# In Christ

# I Am Declared

# Righteous

*(2 Corinthians 5:21)*

## I Am Declared Righteous.

How often are you right?  How often do you think you are right?  Is there a different answer to those two questions?  What does it take for you to admit you are wrong about something?  How hard is it to take back the wrong you've committed against someone?  How about if that wrong was done against God, can you make it right?

As much as we would like to be right about everything, the truth is there is no one who is right all the time, no not one!  Because of our sin, all of our good deeds and right living will never be enough to make us right with God.  That is why a very important part of our identity in Christ is that we are declared righteous!  As you pray, acknowledge your sin and wrongdoing while thanking God that Jesus was willing to take on your sin so that you could be declared righteous in Christ.  Pray that your life would reflect the righteousness that God has given you.  Pray that the people around you would see in you a righteousness that far exceeds any trace of goodness you may think you have.

### I Am Declared Righteous.

_____

_____

_____

_____

_____

_____

_____

_____

_____

_____

_____

_____

_____

_____

_____

_____

_____

_____

Day Eleven

# In Christ

# I Have

# Been Crucified

(Galatians 2:20)

## I Have Been Crucified.

When you think about where you were before you knew Christ, how often do you think about that transition to being in Christ involving your death? What active part does a dead person usually have in decision-making and life choices? What does being crucified have to do with living by faith? How much of your life does God require in order for Christ to live in you?

For most people, death is something that we don't like to think or talk about. In death we often see the permanent end to something while failing to see the new beginning of something else. In Christ, the old must die in order for the new life to begin. As you pray, ask God to help you surrender to the crucifixion of your old life in order for your new life to begin. Pray that being crucified with Christ would put Him in the decision-making role in your life. Pray that the new life you live would be lived fully for Christ. Pray that the people around you would no longer see the life you lived, but they would see Christ living in you.

## *I Have Been Crucified*.

_____

_____

_____

_____

_____

_____

_____

_____

_____

_____

_____

_____

_____

_____

_____

_____

_____

_____

_____

_____

Day Twelve

# In Christ

# I Have Every

# Spiritual Blessing

(Ephesians 1:3)

### *I Have Every Spiritual Blessing*.

What first comes to your mind when you think of blessing?  Are those thoughts different if you consider spiritual blessings?  How often do you think you have every spiritual blessing that you would desire or need?  How would being  blessed "in the heavenly realms" be different from what you might normally think of blessings to be?  Are there ways that it would be the same?

Far too often when we hear the word blessings, someone is talking about receiving some type of physical possession.  While it is true that "every good and perfect gift comes from above", including all material possessions that would fit that category, how often do you consider the greater blessings that exist for those in Christ?  As you pray, ask God to help you see greater value in the spiritual blessings you receive than you do in temporary ones.  Pray that you would make the most of the spiritual blessings that God has poured out in you.  Pray that you would not be distracted from the greater blessings by the allure of the lesser.

*I Have Every Spiritual Blessing*.

_____

_____

_____

_____

_____

_____

_____

_____

_____

_____

_____

_____

_____

_____

_____

_____

_____

_____

*Day Thirteen*

# In Christ

# I Am

# Chosen

*(Ephesians 1:4)*

## I Am Chosen.

Do you remember the choosing of teams in childhood sporting contests? Were you one that was chosen early or passed over until the captains were left with little choice? Do you ever feel unappreciated or unwanted? How does it feel when you are asked to do something special or chosen to be a part of a prestigious group?

There are probably times when every one of us has felt left out or unwanted. We feel like we are on the outside looking in and wonder what it would be like to be included. In Christ we have the wonderful identity of being chosen by God! As you pray, ask God to help you grasp the great love He has for you. Pray that He would fill you with a sense of value and purpose as one who has been deliberately chosen. Pray for a greater understanding of being chosen by God to be holy and blameless in Christ. Pray for a continued growth in becoming what you already are in God's sight. Pray that the people around you would come to know the joy and fulfillment that is found when you are chosen in Christ.

### *I Am Chosen*.

_____

_____

_____

_____

_____

_____

_____

_____

_____

_____

_____

_____

_____

_____

_____

_____

_____

_____

_____

_____

*Day Fourteen*

# In Christ

# I Am

# Adopted

## (Ephesians 1:5)

### *I Am Adopted*.

How do you feel about the family you are a part of? How do you think they feel about you being part of the family? What do you think your family members would say about your desire for them to be part of the family? What do you think of when you hear the word adoption? How would knowing that you are wanted make you feel?

Most of us know families, perhaps you are one of them, who have gone to great extremes to adopt a child. Their desire and love for that child has no limits and they do whatever it takes to make them part of their family. God has that same abounding love for us that He would spare no expense in adopting us into His family! As you pray, ask God to help you understand the greatness of His love and desire for you. Pray for a greater acceptance of the love God has for you that He longed to adopt you in Christ. Pray that you would value your adoption and live as a true child of God. Pray that the people around you would accept the love God has for them as they see that love expressed in God's adoption of you.

*I Am Adopted*.

_____

_____

_____

_____

_____

_____

_____

_____

_____

_____

_____

_____

_____

_____

_____

_____

_____

_____

_____

Day Fifteen

# In Christ
# I Am
# Redeemed

(Ephesians 1:7-8)

### *I Am Redeemed*.

Have you ever lost something that you had to pay someone else for in order to get it returned to you?  Have you had a car impounded that required you to pay to get it back?  Perhaps a lost or runaway pet that you had to redeem from the pound in order to make it yours again?  How do you feel when you have to pay again for something that had already been yours?  How do you feel when you finally get it back?

While many don't like to admit it, every person belongs to God from the beginning of life due to His role as creator.  Yet each one of us has gone astray and left the home and authority of our Father to serve a different master.  In His great love, God has paid the price to buy us back through the blood of Jesus.  As you pray, thank God for the great desire He has for you to be His child that He would redeem you from the bondage of sin.  Pray that you would experience the fullness of God's grace as one who has been bought back from sin.  Pray that the people around you would accept God's desire to redeem them.

## *I Am Redeemed*.

_____

_____

_____

_____

_____

_____

_____

_____

_____

_____

_____

_____

_____

_____

_____

_____

_____

_____

_____

*Day Sixteen*

# In Christ

# I Am

# Made Alive

## (Ephesians 2:4-5)

### *I Am Made Alive.*

Are there activities or events that you participate in that make you feel more alive than at other times? How often do you think about your sin bringing death into your life? Do you know people who have normal vital signs yet live as if they're dead? Are there times that describes you? How often do you just slide into the motions of doing life without living as one who is fully alive?

Many people develop habits and routines that become so automatic that they slide into a lifestyle that would be described at best as ordinary with no indication of being fully alive. In Christ we have been lifted out of the ordinary and made to be fully alive! As you pray, ask God to help you live as one who is fully alive even in the midst of the normal and ordinary tasks of life. Pray that you would be filled with hope as you realize that when you are dead in your sins, Christ has come to make you alive. Pray for the courage to make the most of being alive in Christ as you interact with people who still need to know Him. Pray that they too would be made alive in Christ.

## *I Am Made Alive*.

_____

_____

_____

_____

_____

_____

_____

_____

_____

_____

_____

_____

_____

_____

_____

_____

_____

_____

_____

_____

*Day Seventeen*

# In Christ
# I Am Seated
# With Him

*(Ephesians 2:6)*

## I Am Seated with Christ.

Where do you like to sit when you attend a concert, movie, or performance? Are you more concerned about where you are seated or about who you are seated with? Who is the most important person that you have ever been seated near? How did that make you feel? How would it make you feel to be invited to a seat of honor at an event?

There have been many times in my prayer ministry travels that I have longed to be seated with the first class passengers as I walk through on my way to coach seating. While that has not yet happened, in Christ I have something better — I have been seated with Christ in the heavenly realms! As you pray, ask God to help you remember that you have been invited and placed in a seat far above any first class accommodations. Pray that you would never lose sight of the eternal reward that belongs to all who are in Christ. Pray for a spirit of humility that would remind you that it is by God's love, not by your goodness, that you have been seated with Christ. Pray that others would also be seated with Christ.

### *I Am Seated With Christ.*

_____

_____

_____

_____

_____

_____

_____

_____

_____

_____

_____

_____

_____

_____

_____

_____

_____

_____

_____

*Day Eighteen*

# In Christ

# I Have Access to

# the Father

*(Ephesians 2:18)*

### *I Have Access to the Father*.

Have you ever tried to reach the top of a company's chain of command in order to resolve a problem? How easy has that been? Did you wish you had an inside connection that would give you access to the top? In your life, how accessible has your father been to you? If you're a parent, how accessible are you to your children? Would they agree?

When things don't go exactly as we had hoped or planned, most of us long for direct access to the person who can make things right. In my life there are many times when things don't go as I planned so it is comforting to know that in Christ I have access to the Father! As you pray, thank God for the access you have to Him and ask that He would help you to maintain your side of that communication. Pray that you would always value the access you have to God through Christ and never forget that the same access is available in Christ for all who would accept it. Pray that you would always trust the counsel of the Father as you go to Him about everything.

*I Have Access to the Father*.

_____

_____

_____

_____

_____

_____

_____

_____

_____

_____

_____

_____

_____

_____

_____

_____

_____

_____

_____

_____

*Day Nineteen*

# In Christ
# I Can Approach
# God with
# Confidence

*(Ephesians 3:12)*

## I Approach God with Confidence.

How comfortable are you in going to a boss or supervisor with a request or suggestion? What types of things would make doing so easier? . . . More difficult? What role does relationship have in your confidence to approach someone? How about if you take someone with you that you know is always listened to?

When you want to talk to someone in authority, it is always nice to know someone with an inside connection. It is also good to know that the one you are approaching will actually take the time to listen. In Christ we have One who goes with us and gives us confidence to approach a listening God! As you pray, ask God to fill you with faith in Jesus. Pray that your faith in Jesus would give you the confidence to approach God as you offer yourself fully to Him. Pray that your relationship with Jesus would help you to trust in a loving God that longs for you to come to Him with all of your praise, requests, and needs. Pray that those around you would look to Jesus for a confidence in approaching God.

### *I Approach God with Confidence*.

_____

_____

_____

_____

_____

_____

_____

_____

_____

_____

_____

_____

_____

_____

_____

_____

_____

_____

Day Twenty

# In Christ

# I Am

# Rescued

(Colossians 1:13)

## I Am Rescued.

Have you ever found yourself in need of being rescued? What were the circumstances? Who would you call if you needed rescued? Why? Does that answer change depending on what you need rescued from? How bad do things have to get before you ask for help?

Some years ago I found myself sitting in my car alongside the interstate late one night with steam billowing from under the hood. I had just finished up several days of teaching and was eager to get home but here I was, stranded in an unfamiliar area and going nowhere. Fortunately, I wasn't far from where I had been teaching so I called the friend I had been staying with and he came to my rescue! As you pray, consider how far from home sin has taken you in your life and thank God for His willingness to come to your rescue in Christ. Pray that you would daily live as one who has been rescued from the dominion of darkness. Pray that the people around you would realize their need for genuine rescue from the dominion of darkness and that they would find that rescue in Jesus.

*I Am Rescued*.

_____

_____

_____

_____

_____

_____

_____

_____

_____

_____

_____

_____

_____

_____

_____

_____

_____

_____

_____

Day Twenty - One

# In Christ

# I Am

# Forgiven

(Colossians 1:14)

## I Am Forgiven.

Is it easy or difficult for you to forgive others? How about forgiving yourself? Are there things that you expect from someone before you are willing to forgive them? What role does repentance play in our forgiveness of others? In our forgiveness from God? Is our willingness to forgive others related to our forgiveness from God? Should it be?

If you haven't figured it out yet I hate to be the one to let the cat out of the bag but people can be mean and cruel, making it difficult to forgive them. When that happens, it is important to remember where we were in relationship with God before we received forgiveness in Christ. As you pray, ask God to help you to turn away from all sin in your life and seek forgiveness from Him. Pray for the courage to forgive yourself and others with the same complete forgiveness that you have in Christ. Pray that you would accept the repentance of others, even when it seems incomplete, with the same eagerness God accepts your repentance. Pray that the people around you would know forgiveness.

## *I Am Forgiven*.

_____

_____

_____

_____

_____

_____

_____

_____

_____

_____

_____

_____

_____

_____

_____

_____

_____

_____

_____

Day Twenty-Two

# In Christ
# I Have His
# Presence
# with Me

(Colossians 1:27)

## I Have Christ In Me.

Are you good at keeping a secret? Are you good at hiding the fact that you even know a secret? Other than your relationship with Jesus, what is the best thing that has ever happened to you? How eager were you to make that known to the people around you? Did everyone understand why you were excited or did it seem to be a mystery to some?

I have titled my blog where I initially post most of my writings "Tom's Treasure", based on the scripture that talks about us having the treasure of Christ held in these jars of clay — our body. I write because God has put His treasure within me and it is my responsibility to share it! As you pray, ask God to help you recognize the great treasure that is yours as one who has Christ in you. Pray that you would make the most of every opportunity that you have to share that treasure with the people around you. Pray that you would always live your life in such a way that the world can see the mystery of Christ in you and be drawn to Him.

## *I Have Christ in Me*.

_____

_____

_____

_____

_____

_____

_____

_____

_____

_____

_____

_____

_____

_____

_____

_____

_____

_____

Day Twenty-Three

# In Christ
# I Am
# Built Up

(Colossians 2:7)

## I Am Built Up.

Have you ever thought about building up your physical body? Have you taken steps to do so? Why or why not? Do you wish you were in better physical shape or condition? What would it take to get there? Is it likely to happen overnight or simply by wishing it were so? Are there other areas of your life that you wish you were stronger in? How much work will you invest to improve?

I often get asked about what drew me to a focus on prayer and the writing of prayer resources. From my perspective, the writing and ministry of prayer that I do are not all that special — they are simply the result of keeping at the work God has called me to do and allowing Him to build me up in Christ! As you pray, ask God to help you be faithful in living out the faith that He has put within you. Pray for the endurance to keep putting in the work that He has for you. Pray that you would always allow Christ to do His work of building you up. Pray that the people around you would notice Christ as you are being built up in Him.

### *I Am Built Up*.

_____

_____

_____

_____

_____

_____

_____

_____

_____

_____

_____

_____

_____

_____

_____

_____

_____

_____

_____

Day Twenty-Four

# In Christ I Have His Fullness

(Colossians 2:10)

## I Have His Fullness.

What are some family traits that you have inherited from your parents? Do people typically say you take after your dad, your mom, or a combination of the two? In what ways are you different from your parents? Would you want your children to be fully like you? Why or why not?

Some time ago I posted a picture of my dad online and the social media site suggested that I tag myself in the picture. To the casual observer, and to some facial recognition algorithms, the fullness of my dad lives in me! While I consider that a great compliment, an even greater compliment would be for the people around me to recognize the fullness of Christ in me! As you pray, ask God to help you express the fullness of Christ in your everyday life. Pray that you would daily live as one carrying the fullness of Christ in you. Pray that all traces of the old you would continue to melt away as the fullness of Christ becomes evident in your life. Pray that the people around you would be drawn to Christ as they see His fullness in you.

## *I Have His Fullness*.

_____

_____

_____

_____

_____

_____

_____

_____

_____

_____

_____

_____

_____

_____

_____

_____

_____

_____

*Day Twenty-Five*

# In Christ
# I Am Free from
# My Sinful Flesh

*(Colossians 2:11)*

**I Am Free from My Sinful Flesh.**

What are some things that you find yourself doing that you wish you didn't do? Have you ever excused your own sinful actions by saying you just can't help it? Are there areas where you feel you are a slave to your body, desires, or thoughts? What do you think it would take to break free from that slavery? How often do you think about being dead to your old way of life?

From the beginning, mankind has been quick to make excuses for sinful behavior. We have all had our own version of "I can't help it, it's not my fault." From Adam blaming Eve, to Eve blaming the serpent, and eventually to both of them blaming God for making them the way He did. While the curse brought about by that initial sin did leave us with flesh bent toward sin, in Christ we are free from that curse! As you pray, ask God to help you make decisions that are not bound by the curse of sin. Pray that you would live as one who is free from your sinful flesh. Pray that the people around you would be found in Christ so they would know freedom from their sinful flesh.

*I Am Free From My Sinful Flesh*.

_____

_____

_____

_____

_____

_____

_____

_____

_____

_____

_____

_____

_____

_____

_____

_____

_____

_____

_____

Day Twenty-Six

# In Christ
# I Am Raised
# From the Dead

(Colossians 2:12)

## I Am Raised From the Dead.

How often do you think about death or dying? Why do you think it is such a hard subject for many people to talk about? How confident are you in the power of God to raise you from the dead? When a loved one dies, what makes the Christian able to grieve in a way that is different than that of the world? What do you appreciate the most about the practice of baptism that God has instructed us in?

Throughout scripture we see God giving His people physical reminders of His commands and promises. When we reach the era of His covenant with the church, we find that He uses the practice of baptism as the point where we die to sin and in Christ we are raised from the dead to walk a new life! As you pray, ask God to give you a greater appreciation for His current work of giving you new life. Pray that your baptism would be a constant reminder of God's power to raise you from the dead. Pray that the people around you would see you as a living example to show them they do not need to remain dead in their sin.

### *I Am Raised From the Dead.*

_____

_____

_____

_____

_____

_____

_____

_____

_____

_____

_____

_____

_____

_____

_____

_____

_____

_____

_____

_____

_____

Day Twenty-Seven

# In Christ

# I Have a Life

# Hidden with Him

(Colossians 3:3)

**I Have a Life Hidden with Christ.**

When was the last time you played a good game of hide-and-seek? What was your best hiding place? What made it so good? When hiding, what are some secrets to being able to blend in with your surroundings? What principles do you think are used in designing effective camouflage clothing? Do you think desert camo would work well on a woodland hunting excursion? Why or why not?

I am not a hunter so as I walk through the major sporting goods stores I am surprised at the many variations of camouflage clothing. The manufacturers, and users, have discovered that if you want to be hidden in an environment then you must become like it as much as possible. I have a life hidden with Him when I put on Christ and become as much like Him as possible! As you pray, ask God to help you focus not on blending in with the world, but on blending in to the image of Christ! Pray that your life would be so hidden in Christ that He is all that others see. Pray that the people around you would be found in Christ so they too would be hidden in Him.

*I Have a Life Hidden With Christ*.

_____

_____

_____

_____

_____

_____

_____

_____

_____

_____

_____

_____

_____

_____

_____

_____

_____

_____

_____

_____

*Day Twenty-Eight*

# In Christ
# I Have a Spirit of
# Power, Love, and
# Self-Discipline

*(2 Timothy 1:7)*

## I Have a Spirit of Power, Love, and Self-Discipline.

Have you ever done something that required more strength than you thought you had? Why do you think God would contrast timidity with the combination of power, love, and self-discipline? Would you consider your natural personality to be more timid or more bold? What would the people closest to you say?

I have lived much of my life afraid of people. I dropped out of college many years ago because I could no longer avoid a mandatory speech class and there was no way I could stand in front of the class and talk. Yet in Christ I have been given a spirit that overcomes the fear and allows me to preach and teach on His behalf! As you pray, ask God to help you to use the spirit He has put within you. Pray that the power He gives you would always be used in combination with love and self-discipline. Pray that you would have the boldness needed to always share Jesus with others. Pray that the people around you would see Jesus and not you.

*I Have a Spirit of Power, Love, and Self-Discipline*.

_____

_____

_____

_____

_____

_____

_____

_____

_____

_____

_____

_____

_____

_____

_____

_____

_____

_____

*Day Twenty-Nine*

# In Christ
# I Have a
# Holy Calling

*(2 Timothy 1:9)*

## I Have a Holy Calling.

What does a "holy calling" look like?  Do you think it has more to do with the task being done or with the attitude and purpose behind it?  Who first comes to your mind when you think of someone having a holy calling?  Does the idea of you having a holy calling come as a surprise?   Does knowing that in Christ you have a holy calling change the way you look at everyday activities?

Often times we tend to look at certain roles within the church as being set apart in a holy calling while the rest of the congregation does work that is less holy.  Yet in scripture we find that every Christian has been called to a holy life!  As you pray, ask God to help you to live up to your holy calling in every activity of your day.  Pray that you would take up your holy calling in the way you live.  Pray that you would not be ashamed to represent Jesus everywhere that you go.   Pray for great wisdom in determining actions that are consistent with living a holy life.  Pray that the people around you would see Jesus clearly as you live out your holy calling.

## *I Have a Holy Calling.*

_____

_____

_____

_____

_____

_____

_____

_____

_____

_____

_____

_____

_____

_____

_____

_____

_____

_____

_____

_____

Day Thirty

# In Christ
# I Have
# a Brother

(Hebrews 2:11)

## I Have a Brother.

Do you have siblings? If so, what has your relationship been with them throughout your life? Do you have people in your life that have become like siblings to you even if they are not blood relatives? What makes them seem like siblings? What kind of brother or sister would your family, or the people around you, say you are? What would you say is the best character trait that a sibling could have?

Having a brother can mean different things to people depending on the relationships they had, or have, within their family. For me, it means we belong together and we share a common set of values and beliefs even if our faithfulness in practicing them is at different levels. As you pray, ask God to help you to appreciate the family you have in Christ. Pray that you would value your identity in the family of God. Pray that you would grow in your faithfulness of practicing the family values and beliefs that are found in Christ. Pray that the people around you would know that they too could be part of this family and have a brother in Christ.

## *I Have a Brother.*

_____

_____

_____

_____

_____

_____

_____

_____

_____

_____

_____

_____

_____

_____

_____

_____

_____

_____

_____

_____

Day Thirty - One

# In Christ
# I Have an
# Understanding
# High Priest

(Hebrews 4:14)

## I Have an Understanding High Priest.

Have you ever been in a situation where someone has represented you before another person? What would be important characteristics you would want in a person who did that? How much would you want them to know and understand about you? Have you ever been accused of something simply because the accuser had absolutely no understanding of your actions or your motives?

If I were to ever find myself in need of legal representation, high on my list of priorities would be to make every effort to find someone who had been in my situation so they would have a greater and more personal understanding. In Christ we have such a person representing us before God. As you pray, thank God for supplying His Son to not only represent you but to live life on earth in a way that you can know He understands you. Pray for a greater trust in Jesus as your intermediary between you and God. Pray that the people around you would turn to Jesus as their understanding high priest.

*I Have an Understanding High Priest.*

_____

_____

_____

_____

_____

_____

_____

_____

_____

_____

_____

_____

_____

_____

_____

_____

_____

_____

_____

_____

Bonus Day

# In Christ

## I Have been

## Given Precious

## Promises

### (2 Peter 1:4)

## I Have been Given Precious Promises.

As you consider the previous thirty-one topics in this book, what have been your favorite promises of identity that you have in Christ? Are there any that surprised you or that you struggle with accepting? What is the greatest promise a person has made to you? Have they kept it? Do you trust God to keep His promises? What things have you learned through this devotional journey?

We live in a culture where broken promises seem to be as common, maybe even more so, than kept promises. I am glad that God has shown Himself trustworthy in my life to keep His promises. I am thankful that in Christ He has given me the precious promises of a new identity and an escape from the consequences of sin. As you pray, ask God to continually grow your trust in His promises. Pray that you would understand and value the precious promises you have in Christ. Pray that you would grasp just how high and wide and deep and great the Father's love is for those who are in Christ. Pray that the people around you would come to know the promises of God.

### *I Have Been Given Precious Promises*.

_____

_____

_____

_____

_____

_____

_____

_____

_____

_____

_____

_____

_____

_____

_____

_____

_____

_____